The UNITED STATES PRESIDENTS

Harry S. TRUMAN

Heidi M.D. Elston

Big Buddy Books

An Imprint of Abdo Publishing
abdopublishing.com

abdopublishing.com

Published by Abdo Publishing, a division of ABDO, PO Box 398166, Minneapolis, Minnesota 55439.
Copyright © 2017 by Abdo Consulting Group, Inc. International copyrights reserved in all countries. No
part of this book may be reproduced in any form without written permission from the publisher. Big Buddy
Books™ is a trademark and logo of Abdo Publishing.

Printed in the United States of America, North Mankato, Minnesota
062016
092016

THIS BOOK CONTAINS
RECYCLED MATERIALS

Design: Sarah DeYoung, Mighty Media, Inc.
Production: Mighty Media, Inc.
Editor: Liz Salzmann
Cover Photograph: Getty Images
Interior Photographs: Alamy (pp. 7, 29); AP Images (p. 25); Corbis (p. 17); Courtesy of Harry S. Truman
    Library (pp. 6, 7, 9, 15, 23); Getty Images (pp. 5, 13, 27); Library of Congress (p. 19); National Park
    Service (pp. 6, 11); US Air Force (p. 21)

Cataloging-in-Publication Data

Names: Elston, Heidi M.D., author.
Title: Harry S. Truman / by Heidi M.D. Elston.
Description: Minneapolis, MN : Abdo Publishing, [2017] | Series: United States
    presidents | Includes bibliographical references and index.
Identifiers: LCCN 2015045520 | ISBN 9781680781199 (lib. bdg.) |
    ISBN 9781680775396 (ebook)
Subjects: LCSH: Truman, Harry S., 1884-1972- --Juvenile literature. 2.
    Presidents--United States--Biography--Juvenile literature. | United States--
    Politics and Government--1945-1953--Juvenile literature.
Classification: DDC 973.918/092092 [B]--dc23
LC record available at http://lccn.loc.gov/2015045520

Contents

Harry S. Truman

Harry S. Truman was the thirty-third president of the United States. As a young man, Truman was a farmer. He then served in the Missouri **National Guard** during **World War I**. After the war, he became a **politician**.

Truman became president in 1944, after President Franklin D. Roosevelt died. As president, Truman had to make hard decisions. The nation was fighting in **World War II**. Truman worked to lead his country through this important time.

Timeline

1884
On May 8, Harry S. Truman was born in Lamar, Missouri.

1919
Truman married Elizabeth "Bess" Wallace.

1918
Truman left the family farm to fight in **World War I**.

1926
Truman was elected **presiding judge** of the Jackson County Court.

1972

On December 26, Harry S. Truman died.

1934

Truman was elected to the US Senate.

1945

President Roosevelt died on April 12, and Truman became president. In August, **World War II** ended.

1948

Truman won the presidential election on November 2.

7

Missouri Boy

Harry S. Truman was born on May 8, 1884, in Lamar, Missouri. He was the son of Martha Young Truman and John Anderson Truman. Harry had a brother, John Vivian, and a sister, Mary Jane. In 1890, the Trumans moved to Independence, Missouri.

★ FAST FACTS ★

Born: May 8, 1884

Wife: Elizabeth "Bess" Wallace (1885–1982)

Children: one

Political Party: Democrat

Age at Inauguration: 60

Years Served: 1945–1953

Vice President: Alben Barkley

Died: December 26, 1972, age 88

John Truman

Martha Truman

Harry finished high school in 1901. He moved to Kansas City, Missouri, to look for work. There, he had several different jobs. After five years, Harry moved to Grandview, Missouri, to help run his grandparents' farm.

In 1917, the United States entered **World War I**. At the time, Harry was still a farmer. He was also in the Missouri **National Guard**.

So, in 1918, Harry went to France. He fought well in several battles. Harry returned home in 1919, after the war ended.

★ DID YOU KNOW? ★

By age 14, Harry had read every book in the public library in Independence, Missouri.

The Truman family
farm in Grandview

Turning to Politics

In the 1920s, Truman turned to **politics**. A powerful politician named Tom Pendergast helped him get started. Truman was elected a Jackson County judge in 1922. Truman also went to law school at night. He felt this would help him in politics.

Truman ran for reelection in 1924 but lost. Then, in 1926, Truman was elected **presiding judge** of the Jackson County Court. Truman did his job well. He became known as an honest politician.

In 1919, Truman married his childhood sweetheart, Elizabeth "Bess" Wallace. Their daughter, Mary Margaret, was their only child.

Senator Truman

In 1934, Truman ran for the US Senate. Pendergast helped again and Truman won the election. Senator Truman soon gained people's respect. He won reelection in 1940.

In 1941, the United States entered **World War II**. Truman worried about government money being spent on the war. He asked the Senate to create a **committee** to stop wasteful spending. This committee helped save the US government about $15 **billion**. Now, Truman was one of America's best-known **politicians**.

In the Senate, Truman was known to be honest and a hard worker.

The 1944 Election

In 1944, President Franklin D. Roosevelt was running for reelection. But, the **Democrats** were worried about his health. If Roosevelt died, his vice president would become president. So, Roosevelt needed a strong **running mate**.

The Democrats chose Truman to be Roosevelt's running mate. But Truman was happy in the Senate. President Roosevelt talked Truman into accepting the **nomination**. Roosevelt and Truman won the election, and Truman became vice president.

President Roosevelt
began his fourth term
on January 20, 1945.

World War II Ends

On April 12, 1945, Vice President Truman learned that President Roosevelt had died. By law, Truman became the next president.

Meanwhile, **World War II** was still going on. Germany had **surrendered**. But America was still at war with Japan.

Truman had to decide whether to use the **atomic bomb** against Japan. Truman warned Japan about the bomb. But Japan refused to surrender.

Truman officially became president just hours after Roosevelt died.

In early August 1945, the United States dropped two **atomic bombs** over Japan. Japan finally **surrendered**. **World War II** was over.

After the war, the Soviet Union started taking over Eastern Europe. Truman feared it would also take over Greece and Turkey.

The war had left Greece and Turkey ruined. Truman wanted to help. So, he created a plan to give these countries money to rebuild.

Other European countries also needed help. US **secretary of state** George Marshall created a plan to help all of Europe rebuild. However, the Soviet Union would not let Eastern European nations receive aid.

A mushroom cloud rose above Nagasaki, Japan, following the drop of an atomic bomb.

Domestic Affairs

President Truman also faced problems in America. In 1946, more than 1 million workers were on strike. Home prices were rising. And the cost of goods such as food, clothes, and automobiles was increasing.

Voters blamed Truman and his fellow **Democrats**. As a result, the **Republicans** won a majority in Congress in the November elections. In 1947, Congress passed the Twenty-Second **Amendment** to the US **Constitution**. It says that each president can serve only two terms.

PRESIDENT TRUMAN'S CABINET

First Term
April 12, 1945–January 20, 1949

- ★ **STATE:** Edward R. Stettinius,
  James F. Byrnes (from July 3, 1945),
  George C. Marshall (from January 21, 1947)
- ★ **TREASURY:** Henry Morgenthau Jr.,
  Frederick M. Vinson (from July 23, 1945),
  John W. Snyder (from June 25, 1946)
- ★ **WAR:** Henry Lewis Stimson,
  Robert P. Patterson
  (from September 27, 1945),
  Kenneth C. Royall (from July 25, 1947)
- ★ **DEFENSE:** James V. Forrestal
  (from September 17, 1947)
- ★ **NAVY:** James V. Forrestal
- ★ **ATTORNEY GENERAL:** Francis Biddle,
  Tom C. Clark (from July 1, 1945)
- ★ **INTERIOR:** Harold L. Ickes,
  Julius A. Krug (from March 18, 1946)
- ★ **AGRICULTURE:** Claude R. Wickard,
  Clinton P. Anderson (from June 30, 1945),
  Charles F. Brannan (from June 2, 1948)

First Term
continued

- ★ **COMMERCE:** Henry A. Wallace,
  W. Averell Harriman
  (from January 28, 1947),
  Charles Sawyer
  (from May 6, 1948)
- ★ **LABOR:** Frances Perkins,
  Lewis B. Schwellenbach
  (from July 1, 1945)

Second Term
January 20, 1949–January 20, 1953

- ★ **STATE:** Dean Acheson
- ★ **TREASURY:** John W. Snyder
- ★ **DEFENSE:** James V. Forrestal,
  Louis A. Johnson (from March 28, 1949),
  George C. Marshall (from September 21, 1950),
  Robert A. Lovett (from September 17, 1951)
- ★ **ATTORNEY GENERAL:** Tom C. Clark,
  J. Howard McGrath (from August 24, 1949)
- ★ **INTERIOR:** Julius A. Krug,
  Oscar L. Chapman (from January 19, 1950)
- ★ **AGRICULTURE:** Charles F. Brannan
- ★ **COMMERCE:** Charles Sawyer
- ★ **LABOR:** Maurice J. Tobin

Political Upset

President Truman ran for reelection in 1948. He ran against **Republican** Thomas Dewey. Many people thought Dewey would win.

But Truman campaigned hard. He gave more than 300 speeches all across the nation.

On November 2, Truman won the election! It was one of the biggest **political** upsets in US history.

★ SUPREME COURT ★ APPOINTMENTS

Harold H. Burton: 1945

Fred M. Vinson: 1946

Tom C. Clark: 1949

Sherman Minton: 1949

The *Chicago Daily Tribune* mistakenly reported that Dewey had won before all the votes were counted.

Foreign Affairs

In August 1949, the Soviet Union tested an **atomic bomb**. Truman worried the Soviet Union would become more powerful than America. So, he decided the United States should make more atomic weapons. The arms race had begun.

Meanwhile, the **Korean War** started on June 25, 1950. North Korea was a **Communist** country. It wanted to take over South Korea. Truman worried about the spread of Communism. He sent US soldiers to help South Korea. The war lasted three years.

More than 50,000 American soldiers died during the Korean War.

Going Home

In 1952, Truman did not run for reelection. In 1953, he returned to Independence, Missouri. There, Truman enjoyed a quiet life with his wife. On December 26, 1972, Harry S. Truman died.

Truman became president at one of the most troubled times in US history. Today, he is best remembered for his leadership at the end of **World War II**.

★ DID YOU KNOW? ★

Truman was the first president to give a speech on television.

The Truman Home in Independence, Missouri, is a national historic site.

Office of the President

Branches of Government

The US government has three branches. They are the executive, legislative, and judicial branches. Each branch has some power over the others. This is called a system of checks and balances.

★ Executive Branch

The executive branch enforces laws. It is made up of the president, the vice president, and the president's cabinet. The president represents the United States around the world. He or she also signs bills into law and leads the military.

★ Legislative Branch

The legislative branch makes laws, maintains the military, and regulates trade. It also has the power to declare war. This branch includes the Senate and the House of Representatives. Together, these two houses form Congress.

★ Judicial Branch

The judicial branch interprets laws. It is made up of district courts, courts of appeals, and the Supreme Court. District courts try cases. Sometimes people disagree with a trial's outcome. Then he or she may appeal. If a court of appeals supports the ruling, a person may appeal to the Supreme Court.

Qualifications for Office

To be president, a candidate must be at least 35 years old. The person must be a natural-born US citizen. He or she must also have lived in the United States for at least 14 years.

Electoral College

The US presidential election is an indirect election. Voters from each state choose electors. These electors represent their state in the Electoral College. Each elector has one electoral vote. Electors cast their vote for the candidate with the highest number of votes from people in their state. A candidate must receive the majority of Electoral College votes to win.

Term of Office

Each president may be elected to two four-year terms. The presidential election is held on the Tuesday after the first Monday in November. The president is sworn in on January 20 of the following year. At that time, he or she takes the oath of office.
It states:

> I do solemnly swear (or affirm) that I will faithfully execute the office of President of the United States, and will to the best of my ability, preserve, protect and defend the Constitution of the United States.

Line of Succession

The Presidential Succession Act of 1947 states who becomes president if the president cannot serve. The vice president is first in the line. Next are the Speaker of the House and the President Pro Tempore of the Senate. It may happen that none of these individuals is able to serve. Then the office falls to the president's cabinet members. They would take office in the order in which each department was created:

Secretary of State

Secretary of the Treasury

Secretary of Defense

Attorney General

Secretary of the Interior

Secretary of Agriculture

Secretary of Commerce

Secretary of Labor

Secretary of Health and Human Services

Secretary of Housing and Urban Development

Secretary of Transportation

Secretary of Energy

Secretary of Education

Secretary of Veterans Affairs

Secretary of Homeland Security

Benefits

★ While in office, the president receives a salary. It is $400,000 per year. He or she lives in the White House. The president also has 24-hour Secret Service protection.

★ The president may travel on a Boeing 747 jet. This special jet is called Air Force One. It can hold 70 passengers. It has kitchens, a dining room, sleeping areas, and more. Air Force One can fly halfway around the world before needing to refuel. It can even refuel in flight!

★ When the president travels by car, he or she uses Cadillac One. It is a Cadillac Deville that has been modified. The car has heavy armor and communications systems. The president may even take Cadillac One along when visiting other countries.

★ The president also travels on a helicopter. It is called Marine One. It may also be taken along when the president visits other countries.

★ Sometimes the president needs to get away with family and friends. Camp David is the official presidential retreat. It is located in Maryland. The US Navy maintains the retreat. The US Marine Corps keeps it secure. The camp offers swimming, tennis, golf, and hiking.

★ When the president leaves office, he or she receives lifetime Secret Service protection. He or she also receives a yearly pension of $203,700. The former president also receives money for office space, supplies, and staff.

PRESIDENTS AND THEIR TERMS

PRESIDENT	PARTY	TOOK OFFICE	LEFT OFFICE	TERMS SERVED	VICE PRESIDENT
George Washington	None	April 30, 1789	March 4, 1797	Two	John Adams
John Adams	Federalist	March 4, 1797	March 4, 1801	One	Thomas Jefferson
Thomas Jefferson	Democratic-Republican	March 4, 1801	March 4, 1809	Two	Aaron Burr, George Clinton
James Madison	Democratic-Republican	March 4, 1809	March 4, 1817	Two	George Clinton, Elbridge Gerry
James Monroe	Democratic-Republican	March 4, 1817	March 4, 1825	Two	Daniel D. Tompkins
John Quincy Adams	Democratic-Republican	March 4, 1825	March 4, 1829	One	John C. Calhoun
Andrew Jackson	Democrat	March 4, 1829	March 4, 1837	Two	John C. Calhoun, Martin Van Buren
Martin Van Buren	Democrat	March 4, 1837	March 4, 1841	One	Richard M. Johnson
William H. Harrison	Whig	March 4, 1841	April 4, 1841	Died During First Term	John Tyler
John Tyler	Whig	April 6, 1841	March 4, 1845	Completed Harrison's Term	Office Vacant
James K. Polk	Democrat	March 4, 1845	March 4, 1849	One	George M. Dallas
Zachary Taylor	Whig	March 5, 1849	July 9, 1850	Died During First Term	Millard Fillmore

PRESIDENT	PARTY	TOOK OFFICE	LEFT OFFICE	TERMS SERVED	VICE PRESIDENT
Millard Fillmore	Whig	July 10, 1850	March 4, 1853	Completed Taylor's Term	Office Vacant
Franklin Pierce	Democrat	March 4, 1853	March 4, 1857	One	William R.D. King
James Buchanan	Democrat	March 4, 1857	March 4, 1861	One	John C. Breckinridge
Abraham Lincoln	Republican	March 4, 1861	April 15, 1865	Served One Term, Died During Second Term	Hannibal Hamlin, Andrew Johnson
Andrew Johnson	Democrat	April 15, 1865	March 4, 1869	Completed Lincoln's Second Term	Office Vacant
Ulysses S. Grant	Republican	March 4, 1869	March 4, 1877	Two	Schuyler Colfax, Henry Wilson
Rutherford B. Hayes	Republican	March 3, 1877	March 4, 1881	One	William A. Wheeler
James A. Garfield	Republican	March 4, 1881	September 19, 1881	Died During First Term	Chester Arthur
Chester Arthur	Republican	September 20, 1881	March 4, 1885	Completed Garfield's Term	Office Vacant
Grover Cleveland	Democrat	March 4, 1885	March 4, 1889	One	Thomas A. Hendricks
Benjamin Harrison	Republican	March 4, 1889	March 4, 1893	One	Levi P. Morton
Grover Cleveland	Democrat	March 4, 1893	March 4, 1897	One	Adlai E. Stevenson
William McKinley	Republican	March 4, 1897	September 14, 1901	Served One Term, Died During Second Term	Garret A. Hobart, Theodore Roosevelt

PRESIDENT	PARTY	TOOK OFFICE	LEFT OFFICE	TERMS SERVED	VICE PRESIDENT
Theodore Roosevelt	Republican	September 14, 1901	March 4, 1909	Completed McKinley's Second Term, Served One Term	Office Vacant, Charles Fairbanks
William Taft	Republican	March 4, 1909	March 4, 1913	One	James S. Sherman
Woodrow Wilson	Democrat	March 4, 1913	March 4, 1921	Two	Thomas R. Marshall
Warren G. Harding	Republican	March 4, 1921	August 2, 1923	Died During First Term	Calvin Coolidge
Calvin Coolidge	Republican	August 3, 1923	March 4, 1929	Completed Harding's Term, Served One Term	Office Vacant, Charles Dawes
Herbert Hoover	Republican	March 4, 1929	March 4, 1933	One	Charles Curtis
Franklin D. Roosevelt	Democrat	March 4, 1933	April 12, 1945	Served Three Terms, Died During Fourth Term	John Nance Garner, Henry A. Wallace, Harry S. Truman
Harry S. Truman	Democrat	April 12, 1945	January 20, 1953	Completed Roosevelt's Fourth Term, Served One Term	Office Vacant, Alben Barkley
Dwight D. Eisenhower	Republican	January 20, 1953	January 20, 1961	Two	Richard Nixon
John F. Kennedy	Democrat	January 20, 1961	November 22, 1963	Died During First Term	Lyndon B. Johnson
Lyndon B. Johnson	Democrat	November 22, 1963	January 20, 1969	Completed Kennedy's Term, Served One Term	Office Vacant, Hubert H. Humphrey
Richard Nixon	Republican	January 20, 1969	August 9, 1974	Completed First Term, Resigned During Second Term	Spiro T. Agnew, Gerald Ford

PRESIDENT	PARTY	TOOK OFFICE	LEFT OFFICE	TERMS SERVED	VICE PRESIDENT
Gerald Ford	Republican	August 9, 1974	January 20, 1977	Completed Nixon's Second Term	Nelson A. Rockefeller
Jimmy Carter	Democrat	January 20, 1977	January 20, 1981	One	Walter Mondale
Ronald Reagan	Republican	January 20, 1981	January 20, 1989	Two	George H.W. Bush
George H.W. Bush	Republican	January 20, 1989	January 20, 1993	One	Dan Quayle
Bill Clinton	Democrat	January 20, 1993	January 20, 2001	Two	Al Gore
George W. Bush	Republican	January 20, 2001	January 20, 2009	Two	Dick Cheney
Barack Obama	Democrat	January 20, 2009	January 20, 2017	Two	Joe Biden

"Every segment of our population and every individual has a right to expect from our government a fair deal." Harry S. Truman

★ WRITE TO THE PRESIDENT ★

You may write to the president at:
The White House
1600 Pennsylvania Avenue NW
Washington, DC 20500

You may e-mail the president at:
comments@whitehouse.gov

37

Glossary

amendment—a change to a country's or a state's constitution.

atomic bomb (uh-TAH-mihk BAHM)—a bomb that uses the energy of atoms. Atoms are tiny particles that make up matter.

billion—a very large number that equals one thousand million.

committee—a group of people chosen to work together to study something or solve a problem.

Communism (KAHM-yuh-nih-zuhm)—a form of government in which all or most land and goods are owned by the state. They are then divided among the people based on need.

constitution (kahnt-stuh-TOO-shuhn)—the basic laws that govern a country or a state.

Democrat—a member of the Democratic political party.

Korean War—a war fought in North and South Korea from 1950 to 1953.

National Guard—one of the voluntary military organizations of the US Army and US Air Force.

nomination—the state of being named as a possible winner.

politics—the art or science of government. Something referring to politics is political. A person who is active in politics is a politician.

presiding judge—the judge that manages the county courts and their schedules.

Republican—a member of the Republican political party.

running mate—someone running for vice president with another person running for president in an election.

secretary of state—a member of the president's cabinet who handles relations with other countries.

surrender—to give up.

World War I—a war fought in Europe from 1914 to 1918.

World War II—a war fought in Europe, Asia, and Africa from 1939 to 1945.

★ WEBSITES ★

To learn more about the US Presidents, visit **booklinks.abdopublishing.com**. These links are routinely monitored and updated to provide the most current information available.

Index